CONTENTS

PREFACE

The main text here is that of a lecture, the first to be commissioned by the Old Vic under the Hubert Henry Davies Fund. With Sir Ralph Richardson in the Chair, I delivered the lecture before a large and splendidly appreciative audience in the Old Vic Theatre. As answering questions would have been difficult, I arranged to meet a number of writers and students of drama at the Arts Council the following night. My replies to questions at this 'seminar' provided me with some of the material included here as Appendices and Discursive Notes. While I have no doubt that here and there this extra material— as distinct from the lecture itself—may not be up-to-the-minute and 'bang on', I have decided after reflection that it is better to leave the whole text as it appeared originally.

J. B. P.

1973

PART ONE

*

THE ART OF THE DRAMATIST

*

THE ART OF THE
DRAMATIST

A dramatist writes for the Theatre. A man who writes to be read and not to be performed is not a dramatist. The dramatist keeps in mind not the printer but a company of actors, not readers but playgoers. He is as closely tied to the Theatre as a chef is to a kitchen. His ultimate object, even though he cannot achieve it by himself, is the creation of something I shall call "dramatic experience." I am not going to attempt to define exactly what I mean by dramatic experience. It would take us all night, and I should need the help of a neurologist, two or three psychologists of conflicting schools, and a metaphysician or two. It is the kind of experience we know in the Theatre. Vague and woolly though this may seem, I believe that some consideration of it can provide us with certain valuable insights into the nature of drama and the art of the dramatist. I also believe that it will help us to avoid many common mistakes about the Theatre, to discover what is sense and what is nonsense in much dramatic theorising, to appreciate, in all its complications and difficulties, the task of the dramatist. If in the next fifty minutes or so I have not made good this promise, then I shall have failed.

3

But no money will be returned; after all, we are in show business here.

The crudest example of this dramatic experience will prove at once to us that it is anything but simple and straightforward. We are in the Theatre Royal, Coketown, watching an old-fashioned melodrama. The heroine— young, beautiful, innocent—has been tied to a railway line. We hear the roar of an approaching express train. Can it be stopped in time? Will she be saved? What do we do? We do nothing except perhaps lean forward a little in our seats and hold our breath. It does not occur to us to rush forward, climb up there and either stop the train or unbind the girl. In fact we know very well that no huge locomotive can have burst its way into the Theatre Royal, that those are no railway lines, and that indeed the prospective victim herself, the wife of the touring actor-manager, is no longer young, beautiful, innocent, and ought to stop playing these parts. We realise that a middle-aged actress is wriggling above some pieces of painted wood while an assistant stage-manager is busy in the wings with a train effect—and if we are in the profession we may even know where he bought the train effect. This explains why we make no attempt to save the heroine. But it does not explain why we still sit there, instead of going for a walk or having a drink, why we even lean forward and hold our breath, why we clap our hands when the heroine is rescued in the nick of time. A rational being from some other planet—and possibly some have already arrived—would conclude that we were out of our minds. And he would be quite right. In the Theatre we *are* out of our ordinary minds. We are

4

deliberately schizophrenic. One part of us is anxiously looking down the railway line on a dark winter's night, while another part is sitting cosily in the stalls of the Theatre Royal, Coketown. We are looking at and listening to people who are known to us as actors and actresses, staying at the Midland, but who are also farmers' beautiful innocent daughters and rich glossy scoundrels from the big city. Everybody and everything on the stage have this double character; they are seen in the strange light and shadow of belief and disbelief; they belong to a heightened reality that we know to be unreal. It is this experience, unlike any other, that I call dramatic experience, and that the Theatre exists to provide for us. I say it is unlike any other experience, but this is not strictly true. It is quite unlike any common experience, but there are certain rare moments in our lives—perhaps when we are physically exhausted but alert in spirit, perhaps when we find ourselves in great danger—when reality itself suddenly turns into dramatic experience, as if the whole world were a giant theatre and all this life a drama, so much play-acting compared with some unknown deeper reality. And I suspect that it is this strange link with these moments of mystical insight that has given the Theatre, no matter how tawdry and trivial it may appear to be, a central place in most civilised societies, and has brought the drama close to religion.

It is in the delicate relation between belief and disbelief, between the dream life of the play and the real life in the play's presentation, that our true dramatic experience has its roots and its being. If the balance is disturbed, the experience loses its unique quality. So, if I go to a theatre to see if a certain actor has the right weight for another part, to discover if the new lighting system is working well, to decide if the second act curtain is too slow, I put myself outside dramatic experience. But we are outside it too, at the other end, if we forget we are in the theatre, like the good lady who during a performance of *Othello*, outraged by the Moor's jealous suspicion, stood up and shouted: "You big black fool—can't you *see*?" When melodramas toured the old mining towns and camps in California and Nevada, we are told the audiences often stormed the stage to rescue the heroine. It is a mistake—and part of a very common mistake about the Theatre—to suppose that audiences so carried away represent an ideal, the drama's ultimate triumph. They may have had an uproariously good evening, as they would have had if they had stormed a saloon to rescue a girl, but it would not have been an evening illuminated by what I call dramatic experience. The essential balance, the crucial inner relation between play and reality, had not been achieved. Let me make the point again, in terms of the actress and the heroine. Polly Brown, the actress, is playing Maggie Smith, the farmer's innocent daughter. If I go, for professional reasons, to observe Polly Brown, caring nothing about Maggie Smith and her misfortunes, I reject true dramatic experience. But if I entirely lose sight of Polly Brown and see and believe only in Maggie Smith, so that there is no actress but only a farmer's daughter, I am still outside dramatic experience. The genuine unique experience comes from Polly-Brown-playing-Maggie-Smith. And this important Polly-Brown-playing-Maggie-Smith-contribution to dramatic ex-

6

perience explains our attitude towards actors and acting. No matter how powerful or enchanting their personalities are, no matter how great their skill, star performers who do not achieve this balance, who are too much Polly Brown or too much Maggie Smith, always leave us dissatisfied. They have not given us the true experience. On the other hand, those who do satisfy us, do give us the experience we want—a Ralph Richardson, a Laurence Olivier, an Edith Evans, a Peggy Ashcroft—are precisely those actors and actresses who are always tremendously themselves and yet at the same time somebody else— Polly-Brown-playing-Maggie-Smith. That is what the Theatre demands if it is to fulfil its peculiar function.

Unless they are small children or simpletons, people attending a play know very well they are sitting in a theatre. One part of their minds never loses sight of this fact. If it did, the balance would be lost, and then there would be no dramatic experience. And if we are always aware of the Theatre and it is essential to the experience that we should be, then the difference between various kinds of theatres, various ways of writing, producing and acting, is a mere matter of convention and taste. It is quite wrong to suppose, as many people appear to do, that one kind of theatre, one way of writing, producing, and acting, succeed in creating the experience when all others fail. We may have our personal preferences, but we must not magnify their importance. All drama rests upon convention. One dramatic convention may please our taste, another offend it; one may add colour and depth to our experience, others bleach and dim it; we have a right to explain, admire, defend our preference;

what we must not do is to declare that one convention alone can offer people the experience they demand. For example, there is now a sharp reaction against the so-called realistic or naturalistic tradition; we have had enough of it, the bright young men tell us; and if they had their way, everything on the stage would remind us that we are in a theatre. But these rebels, for whom I have some sympathy because I like change and experiment myself, only write and talk nonsense when they do not realise, as few of them seem to do, that they are merely proposing to exchange one theatrical convention for another. It is no more than that. Where they go wrong is in assuming that in the realistic or naturalistic tradition the audience is being persuaded that it is not watching a theatrical performance at all. Nonsense!

Let us take an example of the naturalistic tradition at its highest point, in the Moscow Art Theatre productions of Chehov, who had a considerable say in them himself. Now in these productions, which I have seen, immense pains have been taken to suggest, especially by sound effects—the singing or cries of birds, the rumble of a distant train, music offstage, the thud of the axe on the trees—the whole life of the neighbourhood, the world outside the immediate scenes. Why did Chehov and Stanislavsky do this? Just to be realistic, to hide the theatre among so many sights and sounds? Is this a clear case of trying to persuade the audience they were not watching a play? In my opinion, not at all. Chehov's object (for the initial responsibility was his) was to enlarge and, so to speak, orchestrate—and indeed here was a substitute for the old playhouse orchestra playing incidental music—certain effects that were reasonably realistic but were primarily intended to create atmosphere, to heighten the emotion of a scene. When, for example, in Act Four of *The Three Sisters*, we hear the regimental band in the distance, it is not there because regiments must have bands to play them out of a town and this is realism; it is there because the distant fading marching music at once widens and deepens the emptiness and desolation of the sisters' garden. Then what about that famous stage direction in *The Cherry Orchard* which has given producers so much trouble? *Suddenly a distant sound is heard as if from the sky, the sound of a breaking string, which dies away sadly.* Does anybody imagine this is conscientious realism, to remind us that we are in the Russian countryside, where the sound of a breaking string, dying away sadly, is always coming from the sky? It is of course another little piece of orchestration, the last instrument of all, the string-breaking, heart-breaking one.

A scene in which a man in a business suit dictates to a secretary sitting at a typewriter may be as good or bad Theatre as another scene in which eighteen peasants, all with large red circles on their cheeks, salute in chorus the prospect of working on a collective farm. We do not go to the theatre to see an actress pretending to use a typewriter. The typewriter is not the attraction. We may be tired of typewriters but still want to see a play about the kind of people we know. On the other hand, we may have seen too much of this particular convention, and so find it stale and wearisome. This happens to young dramatic critics, chiefly because they are compelled to see too many bad plays in this convention. One of our own critics, after rhapsodising at length over Brecht's elaborate wrestling with the problem of Good and Evil, dismisses as dull, parochial, pointless, the revival of *Mr. Bolfry*, in which Bridie handles the same problem of Good and Evil with fine dramatic economy and adroitness, humour and eloquence. If our critic fails to appreciate these qualities, that is not merely because Bridie is not in the swim and no kudos is to be obtained by praising him, but also because this is a critic who has fallen out of love with one style, one convention, and in love with another. But though he may reasonably admire Brecht's skill and patience as a director, he must keep clear of any theory that asks us to believe that by flattening out play construction, disengaging both actors and audience from being emotionally involved, the drama can become the vehicle of pure thought. Anybody in search of pure thought will be well advised not to sit in a building with a thousand other people, a large company of actors, and an orchestra; better find a quiet corner at home and read a few books. Even a Marxist playwright catering for a Marxist audience is not dealing in thought—and, indeed, why should he when they are all in agreement and he cannot tell them anything they did not know before? Nobody in his senses goes to the theatre to be told what to think. What we enjoy in the theatre is that particular kind of experience I call dramatic experience, to which we contribute by allowing our minds to function on two different levels at the same time. And I suggest that it is when these two are delicately balanced and both are excitedly meeting all demands made upon them, then, and then only, the experience is richly rewarding, exhilarating, perhaps ecstatic.

Although many people must co-operate to provide us with this experience, the prime mover in the enterprise is the dramatist. All the others have something to fasten upon; the dramatist has to conjure his play out of the empty air. There are now more and more people in the world who cannot do anything until somebody else has created something for them to work on. The dramatist belongs to a nobler order of being. His pre-eminence is acknowledged whenever the Theatre is healthy and vital. If the status of the writer is low in a Theatre, it is always a bad Theatre. Whenever a Theatre makes history, you will find that it has its own dramatists prominently associated with it. No matter how brilliant they may be, directors and actors are incapable by themselves of creating a Theatre of the highest class, for such a Theatre must produce important new work to be in the highest class, and that work must bring in the dramatist, as the prime mover. So, if there is anybody in the co-operative undertaking who knows best what should arrive at last on the stage, it is he, the author of the piece. Theatres in which the dramatist's work is seen as so much rough raw material, stuff to be dyed and cut to fit out a manager, director or actor, even if it means turning tragedy into comedy, comedy into farce, are not Theatres the world chooses to honour. They are in the superior sausage-and-luncheon-meat trade.

The dramatist and his colleagues, then, must provide their audiences with this double-impact experience received on two different levels of the mind at the same time.

And in order to do this successfully, the dramatist himself, right from the first, must work double, on two levels at the same time. This is true no matter what theatrical convention he chooses. If he fails on one level or the other, if he cannot establish a true balance between them, then the experience demanded ultimately by his audience will be equally faulty, unsatisfactory, unrewarding. This explains what has puzzled so many people: why good plays are hard to write. Usually one level or another is neglected; both cylinders are not firing. It may demand—and I strongly suspect it does—a type of mind and a temperament that are unusual, an author indeed but an author with a difference, neither better nor worse than the born poet, novelist, essayist, but different. So let us take a closer look at him.

We will assume that the dramatist is working in the familiar theatrical convention of our time and is writing a play about the Jones family in Kensington. He has to think deeply about this Jones family. They must take on life in his imagination. Their joys and sorrows, hopes and fears, are his for the time being. He is in Kensington with them, all of them. He is impatient, irascible, tyrannical, with Mr. Jones; bewildered and loving with Mrs. Jones; susceptible and dreamy with Miss Jones; and impudent and rebellious with young Derek Jones, the Outsider, who cannot look forward to anything because he is so busy looking back in anger. Our dramatist, we may say, is keeping up with the Joneses. Now here he is doing no more than a conscientious novelist would do; indeed, on this level he need not do as much as the novelist must do. But of course this is only half the dramatist's task. He is writing not to be read but to be performed in a theatre. While he lives intensely with those four members of the Jones family, he has also to keep in mind the two actors and the two actresses for whom he is writing parts. No, I must correct that, for it sounds altogether too passive. He must not only be creating characters—these four Joneses, he must also be creating parts—two middle-aged character parts, two straight juveniles. While one half of his mind is brooding over the Joneses' sitting-room in Kensington, the other half must be aware, often quite intensely aware, of a box set with two practicable doors erected on a stage. Side by side with the problems of the Jones family is another and quite different set of problems, not concerned with middle-class London life in the atomic age but with the elaborate technique of theatrical performance. Everything has this double aspect. When Derek Jones finally goads his father into striking him, this is not only a painful crisis in the Jones family, it is also the high point of a scene between two actors that may or may not—and either the dress rehearsal or the week out in Manchester may decide it—bring down the curtain on Act Two.

It simply will not do to assume—as so many people, from the humblest aspirants to writers distinguished in other forms, have assumed—that the dramatist need only concern himself with the Jones family and their fortunes. It will not do because, as we have seen, audiences themselves are not completely involved in the Joneses, never entirely lose sight of the fact that they are in a theatre looking at and listening to actors, and indeed depend upon this double outlook, this double receptiveness, for the unique experience the Theatre can give them. So the dramatist only succeeds by achieving, right from the beginning, this necessary and difficult balance. This explains why so many fine poets or brilliant novelists have failed in the Theatre. They could not adequately undertake the double duty. But it also explains why the artful and experienced Theatre man, who knows all the tricks, often cannot write anything worth our time, money and attention. For he fails on the other level, knowing all about the Theatre but not enough about the Joneses, so that his work seems stale, brittle, false. True drama is created by bringing life to the Theatre, and the Theatre to life. This is hard to achieve. So, as playgoers, too often we have to choose between plays by lively and intelligent minds that are faulty and irritating because they do not give us what we want from the Theatre, failing badly on that level, and plays by adroit and experienced technicians who are merely playing tricks with familiar theatrical material and have made little or no attempt to satisfy us on the other level, where the Joneses have their being. Good drama must be equally satisfying on each level: as character and action and life, on the one hand, and the highly conventional art of the Theatre, on the other. And unless the dramatist works like an organist playing on two keyboards at once, the audience cannot respond as it wishes to respond.

This is true no matter what sort of play the dramatist is writing. I took a conventionally realistic play about ordinary people merely as an easy familiar example. The balance is still essential, the dramatist must work double, if instead of writing about the Jones family in Kensington he is writing about Cleopatra in Egypt or the Troll King in his underground palace. Nor, as I suggested earlier, does his choice of any particular theatrical convention change the nature of his task. He is still compelled to think in terms of the Theatre, to satisfy us on that level as well as on the other, whether he decides that the Joneses' sitting-room shall be a close imitation of one he has seen in Kensington or shall be suggested by white steps and cylinders against a black curtain, whether the Joneses speak in sloppy realistic prose, or in that rather dubious mixture of knockabout slang and purple literary phrases we find in so many American plays now, or in rhymed couplets or Shakespearean blank verse or the much blanker verse favoured by contemporary poetic drama-tists. Let us be clear about this. I am saying that his choice of a theatrical convention does not enable him to escape from this fundamental two-level, double-headed task of his. What I am *not* saying is that it does not matter which convention he chooses. Clearly it does, because he could fail on one level if it represented a theatrical style utterly alien to the audience. A classical Chinese drama-tist might have an astonishing insight into the life of the Jones family, but if he expressed it in the classical Chinese manner, an ordinary Western audience would be too bewildered or too amused to achieve the right response. Again, theatrical conventions change, and what was bold, original, exciting Theatre yesterday may now seem too artificial, tedious, wearisome. We regard dramatic fashions much as we do fashions in dress: we accept and even delight in those remote from us in time but sharply dislike or giggle at styles that have been superseded fairly recently by our own style. It is a pity we no longer have chronological festivals of drama, as we had at Malvern in the early 'Thirties. Then I can remember accepting the conventions and styles of all the centuries except the nineteenth, whose plays, just because they represented a recently banished fashion, seemed absurdly stiff, pompous, clumsy. But, if we make exceptions of the style that merely seems old-fashioned and, of course, any completely alien convention or absolutely new revolutionary one, we can say that a fairly intelligent audience can accept and respond to any style of writing, production and acting, so long as it is true to its own particular conventions, and is reasonably consistent in its demands on the playgoer.

Before we come closer to the dramatist at work, let us look at criticism in the light of our discoveries. We shall see at once that much of it is hopelessly one-sided, based as it is on a wrong idea of what the dramatist is offering and the audience taking. There is first the standard academic criticism of the drama, old-fashioned now but still widely read and respected. Here one of our two essential levels cannot be found at all—the Theatre has vanished. The professors almost persuade us that dramatists are not concerned with theatres and audiences. There are no longer any parts to be acted. The characters become historical figures, real people. "Now what," the professors ask, "was Hamlet doing during those years?" As if we were all private detectives employed by King Claudius! When and where, they wonder, did the Macbeths first meet? And so it goes on. They cannot—or will not—grasp the fact that Hamlet has no existence between the two stage directions *Exit Hamlet* and *Enter Hamlet*, that the Macbeths never had a first meeting because Shakespeare never wrote a scene about it. The dramatist's characters exist in their scenes and nowhere else. When they are not on the stage, they are not anywhere. To discuss them at length as if they were real people may seem a charmingly innocent mistake, bringing these solemn professors into the company of the gold-miners storming the stage to rescue the heroine; and a splendid tribute too to the creative power of the dramatists concerned. But this criticism is not as innocent as it might appear. It is up to something, for which it must be sharply denounced. By concentrating entirely on one level, it is trying to make us overlook the other level entirely. In other words, it is trying to take the dramatist out of the Theatre. "Here is Shakespeare, our greatest poet. Let us pretend he had little or nothing to do with the wicked old painted Theatre where God knows what goes on. *Tut-tut-tut-tut*!" This is Puritanism unscrupulously at work. We cannot tolerate critics willing to give courses of lectures on Shakespeare, Calderon, Molière, Racine, Schiller, Ibsen, Chehov, and Shaw, while pretending that playhouses, actors and actresses are not worthy of their and our attention. Such critics should either accept the Theatre and try to understand it or keep away from dramatists and the drama.

At the other extreme is the type of dramatic criticism that functions almost exclusively on the level of theatrical convention and contrivance, with hardly a glance at the dramatist as both a creator and interpreter of life. "Is it a play?" these critics asked, and if it were an original masterpiece like *The Wild Duck* or *The Cherry Orchard* decided at once that it was not a play. Their idea of a play was some little box of tricks like Sardou's *Diplomacy*, of which nobody in his senses could believe a word. Shaw, who spent years denouncing and deriding criticism, called it all "Sardoodledum." Not that Shaw was entirely innocent, if never ignorant, because for his own purposes he would deliberately confuse the two levels—as, for example, when he said that a romantic play was two short-sighted actors fencing without their spectacles. This won't do, because if it is absurd for a mild short-sighted actor to be D'Artagnan, it is equally absurd for another actor who takes all his opinions from the nearest Conservative newspaper to be Shaw's revolutionary John Tanner. As soon as you confuse the levels like this, it is all confusion and absurdity. This sterile school of criticism long outlasted Shaw's weekly onslaughts. It is not completely unknown even today, and may be found, carefully embalmed, in the more old-fashioned instruction books on How to Write a Play.

Contemporary dramatic criticism avoids both these extremes, is not committed exclusively to either one of the two levels, but even so, as bewildered readers and playgoers must have noticed, does not base its judgments on any generally accepted critical standards. For example, consider what happened to *Look Back in Anger* at the Royal Court Theatre. Most of the morning paper critics said it was worthless. Most of the weekly paper critics said it was a play of unusual quality. Discounting judgments that were merely personal and whimsical—and too much of our criticism now is nothing more than that—this wild discrepancy can be explained by the fact that each set of critics was favouring one of the two levels. On the level of theatrical construction, contrivance, effectiveness, tact,

Look Back in Anger is anything but a good play. It merely repeats itself where it should develop its situations; either it fails to make an important point or makes it at wearisome length; one scene will be wildly unconvincing and the next will be simply a theatrical cliché; any experienced hack playwright could improve it on this level out of all recognition. But such improvement might ruin it altogether on the other level, at which new life is being brought into the Theatre, as the favourable notices told us. For the author had succeeded in doing what established popular playwrights have not even attempted to do—he had captured for the Theatre, as the central figure of his play, a type characteristic of our time, the post-War young rebel without a cause, the type who cannot be satisfied by state welfare and mass communications and yet lacks sufficient intelligence, energy and initiative to discover and advocate a better way of living. And the author has made this character theatrically effective, in spite of the obvious weaknesses of his story and construction, by writing dialogue that exactly caught the tone and temper of a large section of our younger people. You could hear these young people, in the back rows at the Royal Court Theatre, delightedly roaring their approval of lines not remarkable for either wit or wisdom, but important to these playgoers because they expressed, such speeches, in a lively fashion their own feelings of frustration or rebellion. This is good, whatever playgoers of my generation may feel about it, because it brings new life into the Theatre.

What is not good, however, is the notion common now among critics both in London and New York that a heightened or unusual quality of dialogue is sufficient by itself, even though everything else in the piece is inferior or dubious, to lift a play into the highest class. This won't do. The dialogue must be spoken by characters of unusual quality too, and those characters must be involved in an action that seems to us significant and that if possible, and without obtrusive symbolism, makes us feel that it casts a long shadow. We shall never see any good new plays if young playwrights are encouraged to believe that they can succeed simply by writing dialogue that alternates between excessive slangy violence and unlikely highfalutin, as some admired Americans do. The critics make this mistake, I fancy, because they have to sit through so many routine plays and listen to so much poor dialogue. They are like a man who has dined for weeks and weeks on tepid soup, stringy mutton and watery vegetables, and nasty sweet concoctions in little glass dishes. Such a man might well exclaim with delight on being served at last with a helping of pickled herring, "What a change, what a relief!" But just as that helping of pickled herring would not make a good dinner, so too some unusual dialogue does not make *Waiting for Godot* into a good play.

Now let us return to the dramatist who is busy with the Jones family. I have already said that he can choose one of several quite different theatrical conventions to work in. But we must not imagine him collecting, so to speak, a lot of Jones material and then deciding what dramatic form he will give it. He will work on his two levels simultaneously. You might say he sees the Jones family, from the beginning, in terms of the particular convention, form, style, he prefers to use. And he will know, even if nobody else does, that on this level you cannot have everything. The conventions, forms, styles, are by no means inflexible; some blends and compromises are possible; but by and large each has its particular virtues and defects that must be accepted, even though the dramatist will obviously try to minimise the defects while exploiting the virtues of the form. All this may appear banal, but in point of fact its implications are rarely understood either by critics or playgoers. A few examples will show what I mean. Would you like a play in which the action tightly unwinds like a coiled spring and every single speech develops the situation, but a play too in which the characters are all created and exhibited in the round? Yes, you would. So would I. And it can't be done. Large characters in the round need plenty of space and therefore a certain looseness of construction, which immediately rules out any tight economical handling, any action uncoiling like a spring. Take your choice, but don't ask for both at once.

Again, why cannot we have plays in which people of our own time transact their ordinary business with each other in neat economical prose but then under stress of emotion speak in wonderful verse like Hamlet or Cleopatra? Why, indeed? Because there is not time, within the limits of the patience of a Western audience, to blend or fuse the two different conventions into an acceptable whole. Nobody has tried harder than T. S. Eliot—and, whatever the result, we should commend him for it—but it is clear he has been compelled to sacrifice most of his poetry and at the same time to over-simplify, not his own basic ideas, but both character and action, denying us colour, variety, complexity; so that in the end we feel there is less essential *poetry* in his action and his people than we can find in some prose dramas. And now that we have arrived at this term *poetry*, we must try to tidy up a familiar muddle. We use this word in two different ways. We use it to describe verse of a high quality. We also use it in a figurative fashion to describe a certain kind of sensibility or whatever will strongly appeal to it. So, if we say a man has no poetry in his soul, we do not mean that he has nothing in verse there, but that he lacks this sensibility. Again, if we say that *Sailor Beware* is a play without poetry, we may mean that it is not written in verse or that it makes no attempt to charm our poetic sensibility. Now this has led to some confusion. For example, we have frequently been told by critics that our contemporary Theatre needs poetry. But do they mean it needs poetic drama in the old tradition, or more plays, which may be written in our naturalistic convention, that appeal to our poetic sensibility because they have a high imaginative quality? For my part I believe that the second interpretation, the demand that our plays whatever their convention and form should have a higher imaginative quality, will be more helpful to us.

What adds to the confusion here in England is that our greatest poet and our greatest dramatist are one and the same astonishing man. A phenomenal genius arrived at a phenomenal time, when both language and the Theatre were just ripe for him—and we had Shakespeare. The mistake is to suppose that the poet somehow involves the dramatist, that if we can push a poet through the stage door he will begin to write great plays. Look at the evidence. In the nineteenth century nearly all our finest poets, from Coleridge, Byron, Shelley to Tennyson, Browning, Swinburne, tried—and more or less failed. Our greatest poet in this century, Yeats, spent years in the service of a theatre, the Abbey in Dublin, and yet not one of his many plays, in spite of their magnificent poetry, really holds the stage today or stands comparison with the best prose dramas of Synge and O'Casey. What lies behind this long record of failure? The miserable state of the Theatre? In this instance, no. The fact is that by the very exercise of his genius the modern poet turns away from the drama; he looks inward not outward; he tends to be deeply introverted, not extroverted; his mind explores itself, not palaces, senates, markets and taverns. Who was the Elizabethan poet to whom Yeats looked? Not Shakespeare, nor Marlowe, Chapman, Middleton, Dekker, but John Donne, that subtle, metaphysical, self-tormented mind which stayed outside the Theatre. I am not saying that modern poetic drama is impossible. We have witnessed Mr. Eliot's gallant attempt, and Mr. Fry's. We have also been unlucky, as three poets who might have succeeded, Flecker, Rupert Brooke (who was turning towards the drama), and now Dylan Thomas, all died young. What I am saying is that it will not do to over-simplify the problem, to imagine that Shakespeare was not a unique genius but a prototype, to tell us that poets *as* poets can rescue our drama. It is only dramatists, who may or may not be poets, who can serve the Theatre, and even they cannot do it if the Theatre, like ours today, does not organise itself to make the best use of their services. But the proper organisation of the Theatre, though essential to the art of the dramatist, does not lie within the scope of this lecture.

The most recent, perhaps the strongest and certainly the liveliest, advocate of poetic drama is Mr. Walter Kerr, dramatic critic of the *New York Herald-Tribune*, in his book *How Not to Write a Play*. Do not be put off by that rather cheap title. This book, now published over here, should be read. I do not agree with much of it, but I recommend it most warmly. Mr. Kerr's thesis is that the Theatre has lost its hold on the big public and is in danger of extinction, not for the usual reasons that are advanced, but because the serious drama of today not only does not give the public what it wants but does not give the Theatre what it wants, namely, an exciting story, striking characters, heightened speech, plenty of action, colour, gusto. He believes that it is the presence of these essential theatrical qualities in the big American musicals that makes them so popular; it is the absence of them from highbrow prose drama, plays that are static or slow, weighed down with too-obvious "messages" or bogus profundity, filled with grey futile people, that is keeping people away from the so-called serious Theatre. If the audience has been shrinking, he declares, so has the stage—in its activity, its excitement, its size. And the dramatists, nobody else, are to blame. Now here I must point out that like many dramatic critics Mr. Kerr conveniently forgets that the drama is a communal art, that the dramatist is helpless unless he has actors and theatres provided for him. Too often he seems to assume there is nothing between the script and the audience. But on Broadway—and Mr. Kerr writes exclusively in terms of Broadway—there is all the complicated commercial machinery of finance and production between the dramatist and the audience. Mr. Kerr cannot denounce us dramatists for not making a few exciting experiments on Broadway, if it is precisely those plays in which we do make experiments that are never produced on Broadway. He must blame Broadway, with its fantastic costs of production, its hysterical atmosphere of smash hits and flops, its ridiculous dependence upon the judgment of three or four dramatic critics! Is this a world in which any healthy art can flourish?

I agree with Mr. Kerr when he says that too much of our realistic prose drama is slow, tedious, lacking in action, vitality, salty speech. But then he seems to assume that the whole convention is wrong, that it should now be replaced by poetic drama; and with this I do not agree. He fails to recognise the obvious fact that each mode has its own peculiar virtues and defects. For example, rather unscrupulously he compares Shakespeare setting a scene with one line:

"But, soft! What light through yonder window breaks?"

with John van Druten, a cautious realist, taking two pages of staccato naturalistic dialogue to set a scene. But, in the first place, John van Druten is not Shakespeare—and none of the new poetic dramatists will be Shakespeare either, we must remember. Secondly, he does not tell us that the situation he has chosen perfectly suits the poetic dramatist, who, however, because of his medium, often makes very heavy weather of other situations. This is true even of Shakespeare himself. Listen to his Archbishop of York:

My friends and brethren in these great affairs,
I must acquaint you that I have received
New-dated letters from Northumberland;
Their cold intent, tenour, and substance, thus:
Here doth he wish his person, with such powers
As might hold sortance with his quality,
The which he could not levy; whereupon
He is retired, to ripe his growing fortunes,
To Scotland; and concludes in hearty prayers
That your attempts may overlive the hazard
And fearful meeting of their opposite.

Now this pedestrian stuff, containing no memorable beauties of verse, is merely saying in effect: "Gentlemen, I've just heard from Northumberland, who couldn't raise enough men and has gone to Scotland. He wishes you luck but sounds a bit doubtful." The point is, of course, that the realistic prose dramatist finds it hard to express the great emotional moments—and if he is English he will find it harder still because the English prefer to say nothing and not make a scene, which is precisely what the dramatist *has* to make—while the poetic dramatist is happy with such moments but tends to be laborious and pompous in unemotional scenes. And unless the drama is to take leave altogether of any life we recognise, the poetic dramatist will have to find a style not too absurd for these ordinary occasions. Some young genius, for all we know, may be evolving such a style, genuinely poetical but also a flexible theatrical instrument. But obviously it will have to be very different from most admired contemporary verse, for it cannot depend too much upon telescoped images and elaborate associations of ideas and the intro-vert's private symbolism, cannot be too involved and obscure, or nobody will know what the characters are talking about. On the other hand, if it is the kind of verse that audiences can understand at once, the literary pundits will say that it is not really poetry at all, that we are not being offered genuine poetic drama. So this whole business of moving the Theatre from prose to poetry is far more difficult than critics like Mr. Kerr would have us believe.

Let nobody imagine I do not enjoy dramatic poetry, gloriously heightened speech, the magic of great verse. Indeed, my complaint is that too often Shakespeare and the lesser Elizabethans are over-produced and over-acted, so that there is too much between us and the wonderful words. I could do with a great deal less for the eye—for some post-War Shakespearean productions seem to have been designed to be taken over by the Sadlers Wells Ballet—and a great deal more for the ear and the mind. Make certain we have the poetry, I say, and leave something to our imagination—and all those soldiers, dancing girls, crowd scenes to Metro-Goldwyn-Mayer and Vistavision. Let me repeat what needs to be repeated: *we cannot have everything.* If some effects are in, others will be out. In the very first speech of *Richard The Third*, Gloucester tells us he is determined to prove a villain and exactly why and how. And this is admirable in its own convention, in which the dramatist has not to worry about slowly developing an idea and stealthily revealing a character, in which he is free to concentrate on heightened speech and swift dazzling effects. But even Mr. Kerr, imploring us to get a move on, would be both astonished and pained if one of our plays about contemporary life opened in this fashion, with the Vice-Chairman of the Board telling us: "I am a scoundrel. The secretaries hate the shape of my nose. So what? I've just set the Chairman of the Board and the Managing Director against each other." That moves, certainly, and would soon move into the street. One kind of drama shows us everything in a sudden wide fierce light; another kind, belonging to our age, shows us one thing after another with a small, slowly-moving light, as if we were looking at a darkened room with an electric torch. Both can have magic, but it is a different magic. The closely ordered modern prose drama, tied to probability and realistic behaviour, cannot achieve the wild and startling beauty of great poetic drama, but its very construction, to an alert mind, can bring intellectual delight. And it can have poetry, its own poetry, not the poetry of great verse that the reader can share with the playgoer. (And here I must add that if you know this great dramatic verse too well as a reader you may always find yourself more or less dissatisfied when you hear it as a playgoer). No, this is another kind of poetry, not belonging to literature, never discovered by the reader: it is found only in the Theatre, created by the total production there on the stage. Read *The Cherry Orchard* and it seems a mere jumble of odd speeches, but see it lovingly produced and its poetry of the Theatre enchants the mind and melts the heart. In one good modern play after another there are at least moments of this poetry of the Theatre, often all the more moving because, like fruit that has fought for its juices against frost and rain, they have been wrung out of our harshly prosaic circumstances.

Time is nearly up, and I have not given you a single

rule of playwriting. But you will find plenty in books devoted to the subject, especially the older books, which often reduce the whole thing to a neat formula. This will be worthless. But there are volumes of discussion and advice, the work of experienced practitioners like van Druten and Ronald Jeans, that deal with the skill and tact necessary in realistic prose playwriting: these are excellent. Such brief suggestions as I can make will be more broadly based, applying equally to most conventions and styles. To the beginner I say: "Remember, first of all, you cannot offer audiences the dramatic experience I have described, with its unique double impact, unless you yourself work simultaneously on two different levels. Bring life into the Theatre, the Theatre into life. Think in terms of action, for though plays are mostly dialogue, the talk should be moving towards an action. But be wary of seeing playwriting as story-telling; the techniques are so different, this does more harm than good. Assume that the drama of debate is Shaw's copyright, so don't have people sitting around discussing the atom bomb, unless one of them has an atom bomb and proposes to use it. Try to have a continuous and varied series of little dramas within your big drama; the ability to write like this marks the born dramatist. Always try to make your exposition— that is, the business of giving the audience necessary information—itself dramatic. Cut out all that stuff about ringing for tea and mixing drinks—all the great dead wood of the English Theatre. Try to suggest life going on outside your scenes: in poor, thin plays the characters on the stage seem to be the only people left in the world. Unless you are a religious genius, avoid characters that are almost angels and demons. Aim at a constant slight surprise throughout your scenes, but in your main theme arouse and then satisfy the expectations of the audience. Allow for the audience, which has its own part to play, changing your piece a little; but don't permit too much, any running away with everything, for you serve your audience best by being its master.

Finally, just as you must look for new life on one level, you should experiment on the other level, of theatrical form, style, contrivance, to discover what best expresses that life and the bent of your mind. You may have to create a new convention. So Bert Brecht, because of his Marxist outlook, wanted to remove the drama from private life, give it an historical sweep, make it suggest the fate of whole classes, and produced his so-called Epic Theatre, which sacrifices nearly everything I want in a playhouse. If I were beginning again, I would move in the opposite direction, towards more elaborate construction and even greater intimacy, taking a few characters through an intricate and ironic dance of relationships. In order to concentrate on ideas, words, subtly intimate acting, I would make a clean break with our picture-frame stage and all its clutter of canvas, paint, carpets and curtains, leaving designers and sets to the movies. I would write for a theatre-in-the-round, the opposite of the movies both in its costs and its art, the theatre where everything visual, except the close and vivid faces and figures of the players, is left to the imagination. For—and I say it for the last time—we cannot have everything at once, and too often when we think we are adding we are subtracting. To pretend about something, to use the imagination somewhere, heightens and deepens what I have called dramatic experience. And I feel we stand in bitter need of this experience at its best, enlarged, ennobled. As it flashes between those two levels of the mind, often evoking strange and haunting undertones and overtones, whispering that all this life of ours may be a shadow show with a deeper reality behind it, I believe it can refresh and even inspire men and women now lost in bewilderment and frustration.

So much for the art of the dramatist.

PART TWO

*

APPENDICES AND
DISCURSIVE NOTES

*

ONE

DRAMATIC EXPERIENCE

SEE PAGES 3–7

All parents who have taken young children to the theatre must know exactly what I mean by dramatic experience. Very small children who do not understand about theatres are soon frightened by what they see on the stage. They feel it is really happening, and when it is not alarming it is merely dull to them, so that they go to sleep or want to ignore it and play with something. A year later these same children may be able to cling safely to the idea that they are in a theatre, watching people pretend, while excitedly following the action on the stage. Then they are entranced and delighted, a wonderful audience. And it is easy to see why, on this theory. Children are fully responsive on each level. Not only do they appreciate to the full what is happening on the stage (I am assuming of course that what is being performed is suitable for children), but at the same time they are even more intensely conscious than adults are of not being physically involved in the scene, of sitting in the plush seat safely and snugly by the side of Mummy or Nanny. So it may well be that it is the child in us who makes us responsive to this magic.

Men and women who are completely removed from their childhood, who for one reason or another have had to take the child in them and wring its neck, generally dislike the Theatre and are reluctant and unresponsive playgoers.

As the father of five children and the grandfather of many more, I have had to do a great deal of clowning to entertain them. (Perhaps my success as a family entertainer partly explains why I have been able to keep many different kinds of audiences amused). On these occasions, dramatic experience arrives at once. A small girl of five, eager and excited, eyes like lamps, demands that you turn yourself into some fantastic creature of your or her invention. You plunge into the impersonation. What happens? You notice at once a flicker of fear in her eyes as fat comfortable old Grandpa changes into this monster, and there is a note of uncertainty in her encouraging shriek. Overdo the performance at this point, and she backs away from you, might even burst into tears and run. So you make it plain that Grandpa is still there, trying to play the little game she wanted you to play, but keep the fantastic impersonation going too; and then, with any luck, she is happily divided, responds on both levels, and so enjoys true dramatic experience. And there is here, to my mind, the whole Theatre in miniature.

The last play I happened to see, before writing this, was the Old Vic production of *Timon of Athens*, with Sir Ralph Richardson as Timon. It was divided into two acts, the first showing Timon as the princely host, the rich dupe, and ending with his disillusionment, the second displaying him as the misanthrope, the embittered hermit. Act One did not satisfy me because I was responding to it almost entirely on one level. I was not living with Timon; I was too conscious of Richardson's performance. There were special reasons for this: he and I are old friends who have done a good deal of work together in the Theatre; I saw at once that he was making the fullest possible use of certain mannerisms, pushing them to the brink of absurdity, in order to float his way through these early scenes, in which Timon is everybody's dupe, withdrawing most of his weight from the character, hardly identifying himself with it, making this act a mere preparation for the next, when he would discover for us the brooding, half-mad misanthrope. For this sketchy play, which Shakespeare probably roughed out in an ugly mood and then never troubled to complete, presents the leading actor, on whom all depends, with a very tricky problem. Timon is transformed so quickly and ruthlessly that if the actor fully creates and identifies himself with one Timon he is bound to fail in the other. If Timon in Athens captures our imagination, then Timon is exile will lose it, appearing merely an affected bore. Clearly, Richardson, by pushing these mannerisms at us, suggesting a man moving and speaking almost in a trance, had decided to sacrifice the Timon in part one to the Timon would who appear in part two, a sound theatrical conclusion. This explains why in Act One I was more conscious of Richardson's problem and of his possible solution of it than I was of Timon's situation in Athens, why my response was almost entirely on one level. And in Act Two true dramatic experience arrived, for during much of it Timon in his new situation and Richardson's performance, now wonderfully alive, were brought into focus. My mind responded on both levels, eagerly and excitedly, and a poorish play yielded dramatic experience of exceptional quality. But this keen satisfaction, rising to delight, could only have been produced by the response of both levels at once, for I have little or no instinctive sympathy with bankrupt tycoons gnawing roots in caves: it was Timon-in-exile plus Richardson's personality-and-technique that did the trick.

Coleridge, in his introduction to his Lectures on Shakespeare, came near to understanding that the drama offers us a unique type of experience, and made a valuable point when he declared that the mind voluntarily accepts stage-illusion by refusing to judge that it is false. He saw that it is equally wrong to insist upon stage-illusion as actual delusion (a fault he attributes to French criticism) or to deny it altogether, as Dr. Johnson did. He goes on to say:

For, not only are we never absolutely deluded—or anything like it, but the attempt to cause the highest delusion possible, to beings in their senses sitting in a theatre, is a gross fault, incident only to low minds, which, feeling that they cannot affect the heart or head permanently, endeavour to call forth the momentary affections. There ought never to be more pain than is compatible with co-existing pleasure, and to be amply repaid by thought.

Later, he comes even closer:

. . . the appropriate, the never to be too much valued advantage of the theatre, if only the actors were what we know they have been—a delightful, yet most effectual, remedy for this dead palsy of the public mind. What would appear mad or ludicrous in a book, when presented to the sense under the form of reality, and with the truth of nature, supplies a species of actual experience. This is indeed the special privilege of a great actor over a great poet. . . .

But then he misses it, by assuming that it all amounts to our having, after this willing suspension of disbelief, no time to ask questions or to pass judgments, our being taken, as he declares, "by storm." This is, in my view, all too negative. It does not really explain why we feel our experience in the theatre to be different from any other kind of experience. After all, many things take us by storm; and even a willing suspension of disbelief is not uniquely associated with the Theatre. Had he spent more time in the theatre, Coleridge would have realised that it made a far more positive contribution than he supposed, that our response on the level of dramatic convention and technique, our consciousness of assisting in a theatrical presentation, our relation, of which we are always aware, of audience to actor, are as necessary to the experience as our imaginative sympathy with the personages and life of the play. It is the simultaneous double response that makes this experience unlike any other. Not better, not worse—we are not arguing that—but quite different, unique.

TWO

*

ACTING

SEE PAGE 7

Some enlargement here of what I said about leading players might be useful. Perhaps I ought to have pointed out in my lecture that dramatic experience and entertainment are not the same thing. I happen to be very fond of music hall shows—or at least I was before they were filled with gramophone-record-makers and radio and TV "personalities"—but I do not expect from them any dramatic experience. And there are straight theatre productions, often very successful commercially, that should be included, from my point of view, among variety entertainment, from which no true dramatic experience should be expected. They make little or no attempt to demand a response on our two levels. If the plays seem to have any life in them, their star performers will strike them dead five minutes after their first entrance. This is because these performers are no longer acting, functioning on the imaginative level, but are simply exploiting large, forceful, amusing personalities. The situations in the play are mere excuses for various routines that are like music hall or cabaret acts. The personality of somebody like

40

Mr. Robert Morley bursts upon us, shattering the rickety framework of the play, and what follows may be excellent entertainment but it will not offer us any true dramatic experience. One essential level has gone.

On the other hand, a leading player must have a recognisable personality or the other level goes. During the 'Thirties, Miss Carol Goodner, a charming American actress, played many fine parts in the London Theatre. But she always seemed to me so protean, so unrecognisable as herself, that I had to consult the programme to discover who was playing the part. She had everything except, to my mind, a unique Carol-Goodner-ish quality to carry through part after part. She brought to each production everything except some special flavour of her own. And of course there are other fine actresses and actors who have left us with the same impression. Now many people imagine this complete and baffling impersonation and identification to be the supreme height and triumph of acting, which they see as impersonation, an astonishing mimicry. Yet these same people, the majority of our play-goers, never in fact accept such players as star performers, never pack the theatre simply to see them. In practice, though not in theory, they insist upon a recognisable and continuing personality—as I said "precisely those actors and actresses who are always tremendously themselves and yet at the same time somebody else—Polly-Brown-playing-Maggie-Smith." It is our playgoers' practice and not their theory that is right. What they unconsciously demand as playgoers is the double appeal, the double response. They want more than the successful imper-sonation and mimicry of their theory of acting. Their choice of leading players indicates their need for performance-in-terms-of-personality, satisfying them on both levels.

There are of course personal tastes in this matter. We may be more sharply critical on one level than on the other, more aware of what is deficient on one level than on the other. I know a clever actress who declares that Dame Edith Evans never succeeds in creating a character for her because she is always too conscious of Dame Edith's elaborate technique; so that for her the proper balance is never achieved. I do not agree with this, just as I do not agree with similar criticisms of Sir Ralph Richardson, but this would be my own feeling about Sir John Gielgud in modern parts, when I am too conscious of what he is doing along one level at the expense of the other. On the other hand, two fine imaginative actors like Mr. Alec Guinness and Mr. Michael Redgrave perhaps tend to throw the balance too much the other way, sometimes identifying themselves too completely and not allowing us to enjoy them sufficiently on the level of personality-in-performance. But age may have something to do with this. Thus, Mr. Charles Laughton, in spite of his massive talent, never achieved the right balance when he worked in the London Theatre because he was then still too young and his scale was too large for his experience.

A great player, I suggest, is a gifted and striking personality that is yet incomplete and insecure and needs what the Theatre offers, a part, a production, an audience, to give it complete and confident expression. He or she does not simply want to pretend to be somebody else. The impersonators and mimics are not the great players, who may indeed be deficient in these amusing tricks and devices of voice and gesture. (Irving was notoriously limited in this respect). Members of other professions, notably statesmen and lawyers and doctors, have to do a good deal of successful performing, if only to sustain a *persona*, but this is not the acting of the great player in the theatre. The latter is in no way deceiving us—and it is essential that the statesmen, lawyers, doctors, should deceive us—but is deliberately filling a part, a flexible and semi-transparent container, with the essential stuff of his or her personality, which in spite of its brilliant gifts needs some such receptacle. Such a personality is not exhibiting itself but fulfilling itself on the stage before an audience. Therefore it is wrong to suppose, as people so often have done and are almost encouraged to do, that the great player will be even more fascinating and wonderful off the stage than on; it is equally wrong to be surprised, shocked, pained, that his or her private life is unsatisfactory, disorganised, indifferent to standards of good citizenship. There is probably enough will, discipline, earnest and patient application, in the player's life to fit out half-a-dozen exemplary citizens, but it is the Theatre and not society that has first claim upon them. To be a member of society in good standing, a useful committee man, a speaker at official luncheons and dinners, an opener of bazaars, merely puts an additional strain upon a great player, who now has another rôle to play, in daylight too and with no dramatist to supply the dialogue; and if only for this reason (and another is that a leading good citizen is likely to be deficient in artistic courage, of which deficiency the later years of that superb actor, Gerald Du

43

Maurier, offer a mournful example) there is something to be said for the old rogue-and-vagabond notion of the actor. What is beyond question, to my mind, is that the essential character of the great player's personality, insecure and complete outside the Theatre, shiningly complete and secure inside it, confirms the theory of the drama I have outlined here. The dramatist may feel jealous or envious because the audience asks first to be enthralled and dominated by the great player; but this is as it should be, so long as the great player in turn looks to the dramatist as prime mover, demands his essential creation, and does not (see the note on *The Author in the Theatre*) imagine himself to be almost self-sufficient, the unique supreme provider of dramatic experience.

*

THREE

REALISM ON
THE ENGLISH STAGE

SEE PAGES 8–9

Unquestionably, the modern London Theatre owes almost everything, for good or ill, to three people—T. W. Robertson, the dramatist, and the Bancrofts, as actor-managers. Their combined success, first at the little Prince of Wales Theatre and then at the Haymarket, opened a new chapter in theatrical history. The plays Robertson wrote specially for the Bancrofts seemed at the time to be triumphs of naturalism; their enemies called them the "Cup and Saucer School." Short-winded staccato dialogue, still much used by Noël Coward and other writers of light comedy, makes its first appearance in Robertson's plays. It was Robertson, as producer of his own plays (though the term was unknown then), who first insisted upon every movement and piece of "business" being carefully rehearsed, in the fashion we have followed ever since. Before then, leading players rehearsed in a perfunctory fashion, deliberately concealing from their fellow players what they intended to do on the opening night. (I remember seeing a foreign star rehearsing with a bewildered English company in this old style). And it was from Robertson that his friend W. S. Gilbert, who often watched him at work, learnt his severe discipline as a producer. The careful preparation and the increasingly elaborate staging of these Robertson plays could only be undertaken by a management that no longer worked with a stock company and the repertory system (easily handled when your scenes consisted of backcloths and wings and the very minimum of furnishing), but financed, mounted and cast each play in the hope of obtaining a long run. It was the Bancrofts too, successfully playing Robertson, who put in a maximum number of comfortable stalls, cut the programme to start later and finish earlier, in general "elevated and refined the tone of the Theatre" and brought it and themselves, so to speak, into society. From then on, ladies and gentlemen carefully entertained, at eight-thirty every evening *except Sunday*, other ladies and gentlemen. Although members of the lower classes might still cram themselves into the pit and pack the benches in the hot gallery, from now on the stalls paid for and called the tune. The Bancrofts were in, the Crummleses were out. Much that was artificial, absurd, under-rehearsed and over-played, disappeared for ever into the remoter provincial towns, but with it, I suspect, went a swaggering vagabond magic that this careful genteel Theatre could never re-capture.

"It is interesting to recall," writes Bancroft, "the great surprise caused in those days by such simple realistic effects, until then unknown, as the dropping of the autumn leaves throughout the wood scene of the first act, and the driving snow each time the door was opened in the hut."

But this was showmanship, not an attempt to persuade the audience they were not sitting in a theatre. After all, if these same people had been invited to visit Regent's Park specially to see autumn leaves or driving snow, they would have refused to go. What they enjoyed was sitting in the theatre and seeing the leaves falling, the snow effect when the door opened. Moreover, these plays of Robertson's, quite apart from any question of showmanship and giving the audience a surprise or two, really did demand solid box sets and realistic furnishing and plenty of props and effects, because their action did not take place on mysterious blasted heaths or the sea-coast of Bohemia but in scenes more or less familiar to the audience. They were not dramatic poems but prose pieces, as natural as Robertson could make them, of mid-Victorian sentiment, comedy, social satire. They had to be staged in this solid realistic fashion to be workable and effective at all. Sixty years later, Mr. Basil Dean was producing Galsworthy with the same care for realistic detail, and he was quite right to do so, for the kind of play Galsworthy wrote demanded this treatment to be effective. If the play is in the realistic or naturalistic tradition, then the staging, the production, the acting, must remain within that tradition. A critic is entitled to declare that he is tired of this particular theatrical convention, though I think if he were scrupulously truthful he would have to admit he was really bored by having to sit through too many bad examples of it; but he must not try to pretend that somehow it does not belong to the Theatre, that on the stage you can put on a crown or wave a sword but must not pass a cup of tea or light a cigar.

No, it is not the carefully realistic stagers of realistic plays who have been at fault and have done harm to our Theatre. It is the Irvings and Trees and their like who are the villains of this piece. They deliberately confused two quite different conventions, and their bad influence is still lingering. We read to this day admiring references to the elaborate care Irving gave to his Shakespearean productions at the Lyceum, how he enlisted the aid of the Royal Academy and the Society of Antiquaries and the British Museum, all the experts on armour and weapons and historical costume. To do what? Not to present plays like Robertson's *Ours* or *Caste*, realistic pieces about a particular time and place, but to produce plays in another tradition altogether, dramatic poems that belong to no historical period and have no exact locale. To produce Shakespeare as if he were Robertson writing about the Crimean War, is a grave offence against the Theatre. It is taking the imagination out of the imaginative drama. It is turning King Lear and Macbeth and Hamlet into waxworks. By the time we have arrived at real sand for *The Tempest*, real water and gondolas for *The Merchant of Venice*, live rabbits scampering about in Shakespeare's dream forests, the ultimate imbecility has been reached. Two different conventions and traditions have clashed head-on. The Theatre has schizophrenia. And it is this idiocy, not honest realism working within its own convention, that ought to have been bundled out of the Theatre.

FOUR

"DRAMATISTS OF IDEAS"

SEE PAGE 10

If what I say about thought in the Theatre is true, what becomes of us "dramatists of ideas?" I don't know about my colleagues, but I have never claimed to be a "dramatist of ideas". Some years ago, browsing in a New York bookshop, I discovered in one of those books about contemporary drama that I was being attacked and then contemptuously dismissed as a "dramatist of ideas". Shaw, it said, was the real thing, and I was a fraud. The critic—I think it was Mr. Eric Bentley but cannot be sure now—might just as well have compared my beard unfavourably with Shaw's. For Shaw of course is a man apart, a unique case in the Theatre. Out of his own passion for ideas, his intellectual delight in discussion, the masterly debating style he forged for himself, a brisk good-humour that came naturally to him (partly because he was less emotionally committed than most writers) and that is invaluable in high comedy, and a tough knockabout sense of the Theatre, he created a new type of drama. In this he is glorious at his best, tolerable even at his worst. Call him, if it pleases you, a "dramatist of ideas", but keep

49

the term for him, do not throw it around, certainly do not apply it to me. Above all, if we are to keep our sanity, do not hang this label round my neck and then blame me because the colour of it clashes with the suit I am wearing.

It is not egoism, though I am probably crammed with it, that makes me now discuss this subject in terms of my own work. These are the plays I know best, and I still have a fair notion of what I was up to when I wrote them. And no "dramatist of ideas" nonsense came into it. Let us take those plays of mine that were concerned with Time. For some years I was preoccupied with the Time problem—it had in fact always fascinated me, and I happened to be one of the early reviewers of Dunne's *Experiment with Time* and soon came to make his acquaintance—and I wrote about it, exchanged much correspondence about it, discussed it endlessly. Now, as I have pointed out elsewhere, one odd feature of this problem is that it divides people quite sharply into those who feel it is supremely important and cannot help worrying and arguing about it, and those who are irritated by any reference to it and believe, or pretend to believe, that it is not really a problem at all, that we Time-questioners are making a fuss about nothing. Knowing this only too well, I would never have dreamt of trying to use the Theatre to convert people to some particular view of Time I held, nor of turning the playhouse into a lecture hall in which I would explore the intricacies of the problem. Moreover, I had a production company on my hands, was in partnership with the owner of one playhouse, had to rough it in the ordinary commercial Theatre. To be the "dramatist of ideas" here, when the ideas them-

selves were so appallingly complicated and I knew very
well that most critics and playgoers were either not
interested or irritated by them, would be to invite disaster.
Why then write and produce such plays?

The reply is that this whole "dramatist of ideas" approach is wrong. It may work with Shaw, for the reasons
I have suggested, but certainly will not work with me. As
I say in my lecture, the task of the dramatist is to bring
life into the Theatre, the Theatre to life. The Time
problem that fascinated me was part of the life I wanted
to bring into the Theatre. I had no hope of handling it
intellectually, on the level of debate, as Shaw would have
done; but on the other hand, our whole complex of feeling
about Time, whether we are fascinated or irritated by the
problem itself, makes us the willing allies of any dramatist
capable of presenting an action, a series of theatrical
situations, that will release these emotions. Nearly
everybody has felt the savage, tearing ironies of Time, as
I discovered them in the second and third acts of *Time and
the Conways*, or the curious haunting sensation of having
been here before, the basis of my play with that title. I
do not say there is no thought whatever involved in all this,
that it is all pure emotion. What I do say, however, is that
an analysis along these lines only leads to confusion, the
same confusion that follows any talk of "dramatists of
ideas". It is far more rewarding to think along the lines I
suggested in my lecture, those of life and the Theatre, the
two levels. Where I was fortunate—fortunate, that is, if
you happen to like these plays—was in being able to
conceive them effectively on both levels at once, disposing
of the difficulties along the second level, belonging to the

Theatre, at great speed and with reasonable success. (I have told elsewhere how I wrote the second act of *Time and the Conways*, which I realised afterwards offered innumerable traps, without ever stopping to think, at the speed of an easy letter). Given good production, the result is dramatic experience a little different from what one has known before, tinged with our feeling about Time. Similarly, two other plays, experimental along the second level, *Johnson Over Jordan* and *Music at Night*, had in them few "ideas" of the type that the dramatic critics who write books have in mind, ideas that properly belong to articles in weekly and monthly reviews. (When I have those ideas I write articles too). What they aimed at, working pretty hard on both levels, was something quite different. What I wanted them to suggest was life outside Time as we usually know it, the kind of freedom of the fourth dimension that comes to us in a fragmentary fashion in dreams, events out of chronological order, childhood and adult life interrupting each other, all of which can bring a piercing sweetness, a queer poignancy, and, again, dramatic experience a little different from what one has known before. But such intentions have nothing to do with the "ideas" that I am supposed to be the dramatist of.

*

FIVE

THE AUTHOR
IN THE THEATRE

SEE PAGE 11

This reference to the status of the author in the Theatre
needs amplifying. Let me say at once that I have no
personal cause for complaint about the way I have been
treated by my co-workers in the Theatre; but then I was
well-known as a novelist and essayist before I wrote my
first play, I am not shy and shrinking, I am prepared to
express my opinions at all times and on all occasions: any
manager, producer, leading player, who tries to ignore me
in my capacity as author of the piece will have to work
very hard at it. There is, however, a bad tradition in the
commercial English-speaking Theatre that the young
dramatist, who may easily be diffident, must be prepared
to defy. In this tradition the author is some poor little
chap, creeping in and out of rehearsals, waiting to be
noticed, who has put together a lot of stuff that the
management, the producer, the players, out of their experience and superior knowledge, might be able to shape
into something like a play. He may be called upon to add
a few lines or to cut some; otherwise, he had better keep

quiet. And this author will be lucky if his name figures on the bills in anything but the smallest type or if it is mentioned at all in the newspaper advertisements of the play. Now if the author feels that this is how he should be treated, that he is not entitled to claim any higher status, then in my view he is not a dramatist at all. And the Theatre that handles him in this fashion cannot be taken seriously in any account of dramatic art: it is in the entertainment industry, and nothing more.

This bad tradition was largely created by our actor-managers in the nineteenth century, when bohemian hacks would be paid fifty to a hundred pounds to adapt "something from the French" and turn it into an acceptable vehicle for the star. Critics like Shaw, Beerbohm, Archer, attacked this actor-manager system in and out of season, until finally, about fifty years ago, a new type of Theatre emerged, a Theatre not of stars in their vehicles but of authors with names, producers, and the teams of players demanded by the new drama, a Theatre that came to life. During the last few years there have been signs of a return to the actor-manager system, and some critics have loudly welcomed this return, which promised, they told us gleefully, to give the Theatre back to the actor. Such critics could find plenty of allies among the new post-War audiences, largely brought up on the cinema and its star-worship, who were clearly far more interested in leading players and their performances than they were in plays themselves. Now the theory of the drama I have sketched in this lecture should make it clear that I cannot possibly underrate the importance of the purely theatrical element, without which the drama as I understand it cannot exist.

No Theatre, no drama, that is how I see it. Dramatist, producer, players, co-operate to create dramatic experience. If I said now anything to suggest that the dramatist stands alone, with everybody else mere puppets, I would be contradicting everything I have said or implied elsewhere. In short, I am on the actor's side. But that does not mean that I believe, with these new critics, that the Theatre should be "given back" to him, that I favour this return to the actor-manager system. I do not.

Intelligent players, as I have pointed out elsewhere, are generally excellent judges and critics of plays they have seen in performance. But left to themselves—as the actor-manager probably would be—they can rarely be trusted to discover and choose for themselves, among scripts submitted to them, plays of high and unusual quality. Strictly speaking, they are not looking for plays but for fat juicy parts, either like something they have already played with success or satisfying some vague or whimsical desire they happen to have—to appear as a cardinal, a detective, a blind musician, a prince of Ruritania. Even when their taste is excellent, when they can recognise in manuscript a play they ought to do, their feeling of insecurity, their fear of failure (which usually increases with success), will probably tempt them to decide on the safe second-rate. Then sometimes their vanity encourages them to put on obviously inferior plays to prove, so strong is their magic that they can turn anything into successful Theatre. Again, famous and much-honoured players become what we might call Establishment figures, guests at Court functions, Royal Academy banquets, City dinners, thoroughly dependable, sound types, so that they may easily find it embarrassing to be associated with plays that are wickedly satirical, subversive, raffish, the work of men who would not be invited to anything official and important. Finally, a dictator in the Theatre, like dictators elsewhere, will soon be surrounded by people who are afraid to speak their minds, who hide the truth from him, who never challenge him to attempt something original and dangerous. And all these seem to me good reasons why actors should not control the Theatre. The best of them ought to have some say in its management, but its policy should not be entirely in their hands, especially its choice of new plays.

The young dramatist should be warned that even when a Theatre accepts him at his true value, he will still have trouble. Dramatist and players depend upon each other, but like many other people who depend upon each other they do not instinctively pull the same way. Each at heart wants something the other does not want. The final triumph they plan and dream about is not quite an identical occasion. There is always some clash of egos. A tension is always there. But this tension, so long as it is not too great, is an aid rather than a hindrance to dramatic experience. It helps, I think, to give final shape, colour, tone and tempo to what is being presented on the stage. The dramatist, as I have stated, should have the clearest vision of what will be seen finally by the audience, but this is only comparative. What he imagines needs to be checked by what producer and players believe to be possible. If the gap here is immensely wide, if the author's vision of what should be created is hopeless and impossible, then he is not in this instance functioning as a true dramatist.

We are often asked if dramatists should produce their own plays. I have had to do it more than once but never yet, I believe, at my own request, for unlike some of my colleagues, good experienced men of the Theatre too, I hold that is it better if the author of the play leaves its production to somebody else. Bringing another mind to the play is like lighting an object from a new angle, thus obtaining a different view of its structure. And authors are inclined to fall in love with certain scenes, certain speeches, that may need to be modified. Moreover—and this certainly applies to me—a dramatist is rarely as patient and tactful at handling players as an experienced producer is, and he is apt, as I know I am, to become bored or irritated and impatient by hearing the speeches he has written and lived with spoken badly over and over again or delivered simply as groups of words when the actors have only half-memorised them. But this producer, whom I am now preferring to the author as a controller of rehearsals, must feel himself to be the servant of the play as well as the master of its production. He must not see himself, as some *régisseurs* do, as a kind of Napoleon of the Theatre entitled to use everybody and everything as mere means towards expressing his own wonderful personality, which he believes is all the audience cares about. Though he may show occasional flashes of genius, sooner or later this type of supremely egoistical producer stops enlarging the scope of the Theatre and begins cutting it down. He does this because he forgets that it is the dramatist, as I have suggested, who is the essential creator, the prime mover. When a dramatist ceases to fulfil this function, he must be replaced by one who does fulfil it.

*

SIX

THE DRAMATIST
AT WORK

SEE PAGES 11–16

Some notes on the subject might be helpful. Of course I
do not know what happens in the minds of other dramatists. I can attempt to describe only my own processes.
Let us have done with the Jones family, which has already
been worked a bit too hard for the lecture, and simply call
that whole level, representing the life to be brought into
the Theatre, "L". Then the other level, belonging to the
Theatre, we can call "T". I say in my lecture that right
from the first the dramatist must work on L and T at the
same time. This could be misleading. Suppose we divide
the whole creative process into three. In the first stage of
it, you are playing around with the idea. (You may in
fact have to do some genuine research, but you are still
playing around with the idea.) And here there is a great
deal more L than T. Next, in the second period, you
begin planning the play, and now there is more T than L.
Finally, you start writing the piece, and now with any
luck you ought to work on a genuine L-plus-T basis,
functioning on both levels at the same time. You are

simultaneously aware of your characters as personages in the imaginary life you are presenting and as so many parts of various kinds played by actors and actresses in a certain setting. At least, this is what happens to me, and I refuse to believe that other dramatists are quite different.

There must be some difference, of course. For example, I know some dramatists who spend a great deal of time in the second or planning period, whereas in my case it is usually very brief and there have been occasions when it can be said hardly to have come into existence at all. That is, I have not been aware of it as a separate stage of the proceedings. What has happened in these instances is that the first playing-around-with-the-idea period has been unusually long and a good deal of T has come into it, of which T I have not always been conscious. But then the final stage, the writing, has in these instances been exceptionally swift and easy, because I have found the L-plus-T basis at once. When for some reason or other I have found myself with a mass of L stuff, with T absent, so that there has to be a deliberate switching over from L to T, the result has never been so happy. It is when there is a rapid movement between them, L becoming T, T becoming L, that one feels confident, even inspired. Let me give a concrete example, if only as a welcome relief from this suggestion of geometry and algebra. Many people, I have reason to know, were deeply moved by the final scene in *Johnson Over Jordan*. In this scene Johnson, the last of his happy memories having left him, is alone with the figure of Death, who removes the terrifying mask and shows a wise, kind face and tells Johnson it is time for him to go. So Johnson says goodbye to this world, this life, and, a small, lonely, but not ignoble figure, moves towards the vast unknown universe. Now every impressive T effect here—the stage emptying itself first of people and then of furnishings and warm light, the highly dramatic unmasking, the great bare stage, the suggestion of depth behind and then the glitter of stars, the slow walk of the actor, now wearing his bowler and carrying his little bag, as one instrument of the orchestra after another joins in the solemn music—was not something added to what had already been thought out on the L level; it arrived spontaneously at that point on L, was decisively what had to happen on the stage, and so the creation of this finale, for which there were detailed stage directions in the original script, was a successful example of L-plus-T. But remember, I am only claiming credit for my own share. The dramatic experience moving the actual audiences owed much to Mr. Basil Dean's exceptional knowledge and resourcefulness, to the acting of Mr. Richard Ainley as the masked figure and, above all, to Sir Ralph Richardson's wonderful Johnson. Here, however, we are concerned with the dramatist at work.

One member of my little "seminar" at the Arts Council asked if it was advisable to write a play from a careful detailed synopsis. I replied that it was not my own practice and explained why. Synopses of this kind are generally written in cold blood, with what one might call the front of the mind applying itself to the task. My experience is that heat and pressure bring in other parts of the mind, set the imagination to work, put L and T into one focus. Therefore, the dramatist who does more than make use of a brief synopsis as a rough guide and reminder, who ties himself while actually writing to what has been coldly conceived by only part of himself, is not likely to achieve much inspired writing, any great imaginative strokes. And though plays ought to be tidily constructed (which is what the synopsis-man is aiming at) it is more important that they should be imaginative. Moreover, the imagination, the mind working at full pitch, can triumphantly solve technical problems that often baffle the cool planner, who is probably making laborious cross-references from L to T and T to L instead of compelling them to work together. Probably one reason why plays adapted from novels are rarely of high quality is that they can hardly ever be conceived on a true L-plus-T basis. The adapter finds all the L stuff given, and must then carefully add T to it; and this is far from being the L-plus-T I have described.

Another member of the "seminar" seemed to think that my view of the creative process on two levels, as well as my later remarks about the dramatist's characters only existing in the scenes he has written for them, could be successfully challenged by a reference to the fact that Ibsen and other dramatists have made elaborate biographical notes about their characters. But when Ibsen is making these notes he is not writing a play; the creative process has not begun; he is busy in the first period, playing around with the idea, and at this stage it does not matter whether he merely broods over the characters or prefers to write their biographies.

Writing on a true L-plus-T basis, working on both levels at once, often enables one, among other things, to make a virtue out of a necessity. Here is a relatively simple instance. A woman arrives to stay, is carelessly or badly dressed, has not bothered about her appearance, looks unattractive. She goes off to change, and on her return looks a different creature, a dazzling charmer. A writer not functioning on the T level will probably be so eager to show what happens after the transformation that he will not allow the actress sufficient time to re-do her hair and face and change her clothes, even if she is using a quick-changing room in the wings. The old T hand will not make this mistake; he will probably earn the actress's gratitude by allowing her plenty of time; but while acknowledging the necessity he will probably not make a virtue of it, will not succeed in elaborating or strengthening the situation on the stage while the actress is off, changing. But if he is able to work with L-plus-T, it is more than likely that instead of keeping things merely ticking over while the actress is changing he will realise that he can use these ten minutes to make the scene of her re-entrance far more effective than it might have been. But "realise" is probably misleading in these circumstances; it suggests—at least, to me—a problem spread out and reflected upon; but his mind will not be working in that fashion; he will probably have made a virtue out of this necessity without knowing he was doing it, one half of his mind timing the actress's change, the other half swiftly building up the scene during her absence.

Finally, what about writing parts for certain players? I am so far from being opposed to it that I consider the absence of this opportunity one of the weaknesses of the London Theatre, in which new plays are rarely performed by stock companies. Writing parts for certain players must not be confused with something quite different, namely, the old hack practice of providing, usually at their suggestion, actor-managers with "vehicles." Here the author does not write the play *he* wants to write but the one the actor-manager demands that he should write. He is doing not a creative but a catering job. But a man may be writing parts with certain players in mind, and creating a dramatic masterpiece. What was good enough for almost every great dramatist from Shakespeare to Chehov (see his letters) is good enough for the rest of us. On the comparatively few occasions when I have been able to follow their example—for the improvised producing of the London Theatre makes it almost impossible —I have found it challenging, stimulating and finally rewarding. It helps, I have noticed, on both levels, even though it belongs itself entirely to T. But while I would be happy working with a stock company, it would have to be a large one (offering me, let us say, a choice of thirty players for ten characters), much larger, indeed, than the present economics of our Theatre would allow. Nevertheless, even on our commercial basis, with all its necessary economies, whenever a management has adopted a definite policy and has built up a company to interpret that policy, it has begun to achieve something instead of floundering around. Thus, the old Aldwych farces were no masterpieces of wit and humour, and the company, almost a stock company, that played them was not blazing with great talent, but these Aldwych productions had a pleasant and profitable place in the London life of the 'Twenties, are remembered with gratitude when hundreds of theatrical enterprises have been forgotten, just because a policy and a playhouse and an author and a copmany for once were closely and securely linked. Theatre work in any circumstances can hardly escape being difficult and precarious, but now we have made it ten times more difficult and precarious than it need be. Much of the energy and attention that ought to be given to the work is wasted now looking for and making sure of the work. The Theatre has sufficient problems of its own without our putting it at the end of an obstacle race.

SEVEN

DONS AND THE DRAMA

SEE PAGES 16–17

There are some additions I should like to make to my remarks in the lecture about the professors. If I had my way the drama would be taken out of Eng. Lit. or any other Lit., except perhaps Greek, at our universities. What we need is what so many American universities have, namely, a separate Drama School that has its own theatre, a real theatre producing plays that audiences pay to see. Even if such a Drama School should have courses in play-writing, little harm will be done so long as the theatre itself is just round the corner. An excellent foundation for future good work in the Theatre can be laid in a school of this sort. But I for one am deeply suspicious of the Eng. Lit. approach to drama. Courses of lectures are often given by dons who pride themselves upon rarely going near a playhouse. They may pass on a certain amount of useful information and make an occasional point or two, but their general influence is more likely to be bad than good. They are examining and judging drama in the wrong atmosphere: the fish is out of water and is dying. Most of them would enthusiastically agree with Henry James (a first favourite) when he writes to his brother: "The whole odiousness of the thing lies in the connection between the drama and the theatre. The one is admirable in its interest and difficulty, the other loathsome in its conditions . . ." Here the cat is out of the bag.

Most of us who write for it have cursed the Theatre longer and louder than Henry James did. We have damned the whole mob of them—players, producers, designers, managers, theatre owners, box office managers, library (ticket agency) dealers, audiences and all. We have probably told ourselves that never again will we write a play for these imbeciles. We have sat up until dawn, shivering, yawning, hungry but half-sick with smoking too much, trying to make some of them see reason. We have rehearsed and re-written, re-written and re-hearsed, until the play seemed to lose all sense and meaning. And even in our calmer and more hopeful moments we have known only too well that the Theatre, here or anywhere else, ought to have its whole organisation torn to pieces and then carefully put together again. We have used up pounds and pounds of tobacco and cases of whisky deciding how the Theatre ought to be reformed. Of course the thing is odious, loathsome, a dramatist's nightmare and heartbreak. Whatever Henry James says about it, I am ready to double and re-double. But he must not try to take the drama away from it. This is quite as absurd as trying to take the symphony away from the orchestra and the concert hall. If there is no Theatre, then there is no drama, only something else to read. If the Theatre is too demanding, too coarse and vulgar, altogether repugnant, then the drama is not for you. Of course it can be vastly improved, its whole convention can be changed, but it remains the Theatre, where actors perform on a stage of some sort and an audience sits in silence when it is enthralled, laughs when it is tickled, coughs when it is bored. And no matter how strong and original the dramatist's genius, he will have to come to terms with it or he will not be a dramatist.

This is what the typical Eng. Lit. critic of the drama tries to deny. Because he will not accept the Theatre, keeps the dramatist in the library, does not understand what I have called dramatic experience, his values and judgments are all over the place. The opinion of any fairly intelligent actor or actress is far sounder than that of most of these learned critics. It is the Eng. Lit. approach that does the mischief. And I cannot help feeling that the contemporary English Theatre has suffered to some extent from the influence of these university critics. (With a possible couple of exceptions at Oxford and Cambridge). For considerable numbers of intelligent young men and women, prepared to be deeply interested in the Theatre, perhaps to work for it, have had their values and tastes addled by a course or two of lectures on the drama disconnected with the Theatre. So, I repeat, our universities should either establish proper Drama Schools with their own playhouses or ignore the whole subject as a separate piece of study.

EIGHT

*

BROADWAY

SEE PAGES 24–25

Some further remarks about Broadway are badly needed here. Everybody must have noticed that successful Broadway productions enjoy a prestige throughout the Western World that they never had before, not even just before the War. Is this because Broadway now has the best dramatists, the best directors and actors, the best critics and playgoers? This is often assumed to be the case, especially by American theatre people and journalists; it is in my opinion an unwarranted assumption. There is of course plenty of fine talent in and around Broadway. And it has, I suspect, far more playgoers who really want good new plays than London has. (I am referring now to the small public that makes dramatic hits, not the mob that swarms in afterwards, following fashion; and both in New York and London this public is surprisingly small, and in London is smaller than it used to be). But there are two reasons why Broadway now enjoys such enormous prestige. First, because America itself is accepted as the richest and most powerful country in the world. Its values and standards are now accepted by more and more people outside America. It is regarded as the military, economic, and (in spite of many denials that should be regarded with suspicion) social and cultural leader of the Western World. And Broadway is the theatrical Mecca of this vast glittering continent. It is linked with Hollywood, which still commands most of our screens in Western Europe and elsewhere, which can show us cheques for a million dollars being handed over for the motion picture rights of a successful Broadway show. How pitiful, after that, our own little transactions in pounds sterling, francs, lire and pesetas seem to us! Size, power, wealth, all are there. And publicity on a scale hitherto unknown. This brings us to the second reason. American magazines like *Time*, *Life* and the rest are now published and widely read in country after country, so that more and more people in more and more places learn about Broadway's latest smash hit. Musicals of no exceptional merit are eagerly acquired and slavishly reproduced in capital after capital. Plays known to have earned fortunes on Broadway are regarded as masterpieces of world Theatre. For it is difficult to resist, especially in the uncertain and insecure world of show business, the weight and thrust of such publicity.

Let us take a particular example of how it works. As I write this, Mr. Arthur Miller has had his last play successfully produced by a new Theatre Club in London, and both Mr. Miller and his play have received from our press, radio and TV an amount of attention rarely given to anybody and anything connected with the Theatre. Here I must add that no hostile criticism of Mr. Miller himself is intended; his plays are good plays, well worth producing anywhere; he is a writer with exceptional intelligence and integrity; he has conducted himself, in a difficult situation, with an admirable good sense that the rest of us might well envy. The fact remains, however, that he finds himself in this blaze of publicity because he arrived here as the husband of Miss Marilyn Monroe, famous throughout the world, thanks to Hollywood publicity methods, as a fabulous "pin-up" film star, whose every movement is regarded (for reasons best known to themselves and rather mysterious to many of us) as front page news even by British newspapers. It cannot be denied that he owes all this immediate excited attention less to his own considerable gifts than to the influence of Broadway, Hollywood and ubiquitous American journalism. This is not his fault; nobody is blaming him. But this is an example of how what might almost be called the "American propaganda machine" gets to work on us.

Now the chief danger here for us is that, unless we know better, we shall accept Broadway as standard Theatre. This is in fact what Mr. Kerr does in his book. He assumes that the Theatre as he knows it in Broadway is the Theatre of our time and world. It is nothing of the kind. Many of his criticisms do not apply to the Theatre elsewhere. Of this I gave an example in my lecture when I pointed out that he could not blame us for not making experiments when it is in fact our experimental plays that are never produced on Broadway. (For instance, among plays of mine that have never been produced on Broadway are *Johnson Over Jordan*, *Music at Night*, *Desert Highway*, *They Came to a City*, *Ever Since Paradise*, *Summer Day's Dream*, and now, so far offered in vain, *Take the Fool Away*. I do not say Mr. Kerr would have liked these plays if he had seen them. But at least he could hardly have accused me of doing the same old thing in the same old way). As I said in my review of his book, Mr. Kerr does not take into account the fantastic conditions and climate of Broadway. For even the slow, dismal, bogus-profound plays he denounces are an inevitable product, through a reaction against brash and falsely bright commercial playwriting, of an unhealthy atmosphere, wrong attitudes, bad conditions, the "smash hit or flop" Theatre, depending for its life on the opinions of three or four critics. It is simply idiotic that the production of a straight play, with one set and a small cast, can cost £80,000, and then, because Mr. Kerr and two or three of his colleagues do not happen to like it, be taken off after a few nights. This is the Theatre in a madhouse. Plays should not cost this sort of money to produce; they should not be hastily judged to be either world-beaters or garbage for the ashcan; the Theatre is not improved by everybody in it having a high temperature or behaving as if they were at the gaming tables at two in the morning; and what is needed is not more and more money, brighter and brighter lights, bolder ticket scalpers, more and more ballyhoo, a still sharper division of playwrights into geniuses and morons, more and more productions either closing after three nights or selling out for three years, more and more silliness and hysteria. What would happen to music and painting if composers and artists had to live and work in such an atmosphere? What would happen to books if each one cost £100,000 to publish and made either a million or a dead loss?

Two types of plays flourish best in this Broadway climate One is the streamlined, waterproofed, enamel-finish, cellophane-wrapped article of theatrical merchandise. These are put together by several people, just as most films are. (Hollywood borrowed this practice from Broadway.) After the piece has gone on the road, it is re-written again and again. A leading character can be suffering from an incurable disease in Philadelphia, be gravely ill in Boston, merely threatened with illness in New Haven, and not even be out of sorts when the play finally arrives on 42nd Street. I am not denying that this trial-and-error method produces some excellent entertainment—it is particularly good for farce—but it is unlikely to achieve any great drama. Much greater claims are made for the other type of play, associated with authors of considerable talent— for example, Tennessee Williams' prize-winning smash hit, *Cat on a Hot Tin Roof*, which has been raved about as if it were another *King Lear*. While in no doubt whatever about this dramatist's originality and power, I venture to suggest that Broadway does him more harm than good. It encourages him to indulge in false violence, to give everybody a shot in the arm, to write whole scenes at the top of his voice, to bounce and stun the audience into admiring his treatment of characters and situations neither very original nor very subtle. There is always a danger that playgoers coming out of the glare and din of Broadway will find everything but the strongest stuff an anti-climax in the theatre, so Mr. Williams gives them the full treatment—cancer, alcoholism, homosexuality, impotence, the whole screaming works. My own theory prevents my passing any judgment here, for this is a play I have read carefully but have not yet seen. Thus I do not know what kind of dramatic experience it offers us in the theatre, even though its assault on the nerves is not hard to imagine. But what I dislike or am suspicious of in reading the play seems to me to suggest the Broadway influence rather than any fundamental flaw in the dramatist. Let us hope that all our theatrical bouquets will not soon consist entirely of brilliant blooms from this hot-house.

NINE

THE ENGLISH
AND THE THEATRE

SEE PAGE 26

A few notes on that remark in parenthesis—*"and if he is English he will find it harder still because the English prefer to say nothing and not make a scene, which is precisely what the dramatist* has *to make."* Critics rarely seem to realise how difficult it is for a dramatist working in the realistic convention to write a highly theatrical and richly coloured play about contemporary English people. The trouble is that, unlike the almost hysterically dramatic Americans, the imaginatively articulate Irish, the pointed and witty French, the English are not on the dramatist's side. They do their best to avoid a scene. All their drama is hidden away inside their heads, lost in their secret dreams. Just when they ought to speak out, either they mumble some commonplace or walk away. Their characteristic speech is anything but picturesque and dramatic. It is as if you had to devise a whole banquet out of rice pudding and stewed pears. Weary of such fare, as well they might be, our younger critics are now demanding dialogue that has plenty of colour, clang, thrust and glitter. Fair enough.

74

Even some of us older hands—to say nothing of the younger and more eager authors—are not hopelessly incapable of writing such dialogue. But how are we to do it and yet at the same time present recognisable contemporary English figures? Clearly some of our younger dramatists are avoiding this dilemma by going into the past, by setting their scene in Ruritania or one of its neighbours, by abandoning realism altogether. One can hardly blame them. That may be the best way out. Nevertheless, some plays demand to be written in terms of fairly characteristic contemporary English people, and if they are to behave and talk as such people do, then the dramatist has a horribly difficult problem to face. After grappling with it for a quarter of a century, I am ready to maintain that dramatists elsewhere, the Americans, the Irish, the French and the rest, are very lucky fellows, who do not know what a theatrical obstacle race can do to them.

For example. Just after the war I wrote a play about a middle-class English family that I called *The Linden Tree*. Now it would not have been beyond my contrivance and wit to have created a family of highly articulate and passionate eccentrics, who between them might have worked up the most extraordinary scenes blazing with the kind of dialogue our younger critics tell us is essential to the Theatre. But this would not have been the play I wanted to write, a play about a family that might be found not too far from any provincial university. Those highly articulate and passionate eccentrics simply would not be the Lindens. If I let rip, aiming entirely at immediate theatrical effect, I lose the particular situation I want to

75

present. Unless we recognise and accept the Lindens, we may be vastly entertained, but nothing, in the sense in which I conceived the play, comes home to us. No Lindens, no play. Given such a family, my problem then is how to make them as dramatic and articulate as possible —perhaps always the major problem, the grand headache, of any English dramatist who has not forsworn realism altogether. I solve it, so far as I am able to solve it, by a multitude of sleights and devices. Old Linden is a professor, able therefore to express himself with some vigour and warmth, especially as he is under the threat of compulsory retirement. I am not good at likeable young girls (I make them too arch), but I risk giving him a youngest daughter still at home and learning the 'cello, because she will loosen him up still more. Mrs. Linden can explode because she is at the end of her tether. The "help" can be a bit mad; they often are. The other three Linden children return home from three entirely different styles of life, and each brings a certain amount of combustible or explosive material. It is in intimate family scenes that the English middle-classes are most likely to let themselves go, to unstiffen upper lips, especially if they have been away from home and memories of their childhood return with a rush. So we must see the Lindens, as a family, trying to celebrate something. I could go on and on, showing how this problem of making the contemporary English theatrically effective has to be tackled in a hundred different ways, but will content myself with one final and important point. In this play—as in several others of mine—I open with absolutely realistic flat dialogue of the kind that any English audience knows only too well, and then gradually I begin to move away from complete naturalism in speech, so that in the last half-hour the characters are using a far richer and warmer idiom, often making speeches that would be impossible to them in real life. I have done this over and over again—and nobody has ever noticed it.

But if middle-class English life is so unhelpful to the dramatist, why not leave it alone and go up or down in the social scale? Dukes or dustmen. The answer is that a realistic dramatist, writing about contemporary England, would not be better served outside the middle-classes. If he went back fifty or a hundred years, he could probably find racy speech both at the top and the bottom of the social ladder; but not today. From a dramatist's point of view, all the English today speak badly. Their talk lacks invention and zest, warmth and colour. Most of them sound bored, which indeed is what they are. What this means is that an English dramatist, wanting to present his own people realistically, will have to work about twice as hard to create genuine drama as dramatists in other countries have to do. However, some exquisite flowers often burst out of unpromising soil.

*

TEN

SHAKESPEARE

HOW TO RUIN HIM

AND HOW TO USE HIM

TO WRECK THE ENGLISH THEATRE

SEE PAGES 25–28

Much of our traffic with Shakespeare since the war might be described as a comedy of errors and love's labours lost. We come to bury Shakespeare not to praise him, to bury him beneath a vast load of scenery, costumes and props. We choose his works because the best of them are great dramatic poems, and then proceed, to almost everybody's gratification and delight, to treat them as if they were anything but great dramatic poems. Strongly visual producers, with one eye on the ballet, are especially invited to take charge of Shakespeare, and if they cut some of his best lines to make time for the arrival of more dancing girls, trumpeters, courtiers and mixed citizens, nobody cares. More than once, at the end of a school summer term, I have sweltered at the back of the gymnasium and have listened to the lovely lines come piping out through

78

cottonwool moustaches and beards, and have felt far closer to Shakespeare's heart and mind than I have done while attending some of the most elaborate professional productions. The trouble is that in so many of these productions they will not let the words do the work. They do not trust the words. They imagine that poetry is not value for money. So everything else that is not poetry is overdone. Or let me put it this way. The mistake is to suppose that a Shakespearean play is not a particular kind of play, devised for a certain kind of theatre, aiming at certain kinds of effects, but a sort of vast Christmas hamper of drama out of which can be brought everything for everybody: with the result that too often what is wonderful, miraculous, in Shakespeare can be lost in the huge bewildering mess of paint, canvas, woodwork, false hair, silk and satin, weapons and armour, ballet dancing, processions, imitation lutes and trumpets, the real orchestra down below, and players all acting their heads off. And audiences are so busy taking it all in, getting their money's worth, that the enchanting words slip by unnoticed. So everybody concerned with the production has had a roaring good time except the essential spirit of Shakespeare.

At the risk of appearing thoroughly ungrateful to the sponsors of this lecture, I will venture some further observations. The policy of diverting most of the funds intended to keep the Theatre alive into Shakespearean production is quite wrong. Shakespeare does not need the money, which only encourages too elaborate and too costly methods of production, not only unnecessary but downright harmful. Produced as he ought to be produced,

Shakespeare will easily pay his way. *Hamlet* and *Othello* have been packing pits and galleries for centuries. It is contemporary drama of the more serious and experimental sort that urgently needs subsidising, just because it is unlikely to pay its way at first and is a dubious commercial asset. Countries with heavily subsidised national or municipal theatres do not confine themselves to reviving the classics but are able to offer the modern dramatist an opportunity to break away from what is merely fashionable and commercially sound. As a dramatist who has been in this position abroad, I have found it difficult to make Theatre people there understand what happens in London. As it is, at one and the same time we are actually ruining Shakespeare by not producing him properly, and using him to wreck our contemporary Theatre. If a similar system had been at work during the later years of Elizabeth's reign, we would never have had a Shakespeare. Again, if I thought that this concentration on the Bard was the result of a great new passion for dramatic poetry, I would be happier about it, but, as we have seen, too often it is the poetry that suffers. I do not believe that Shakespeare the bawdy comic poet and the savagely tragic poet is taking hold of post-War England. It is Shakespeare the cultural monument, the safe figure, the dramatist who will not disturb you with strange subversive ideas, the Establishment author, who is in favour. What is wrong with so many of us is not that we do not write as well as Shakespeare (no one knows this better than we do) but that we are still alive.

Another mistaken policy is to confine our subsidised tours abroad entirely to productions of Shakespeare. The official idea is that other countries only want Shakespeare from us. That is not my experience, and I regularly see something of Theatre people abroad. They produce Shakespeare too, and though naturally they are ready to welcome and to admire players like Dame Peggy Ashcroft and Sir John Gielgud, they do not think we present Shakespeare any better than they do. And if they are Central Europeans, they know that we have far more contemporary dramatists than they have, more plays about the world we are all living in, and they cannot help wondering what we are doing with these dramatists and these plays. They do not believe that, for all his universal genius, the Theatre begins and ends with Shakespeare. And neither do I.

Although we have seen some magnificent Shakespearean performances during the past ten years, we ought to regard this post-War bardolatry with suspicion. There is something routine, official, tired, about it. The contemporary Theatre is losing, but Shakespeare is not winning. What is really happening is that most of the excitement it should have is being taken out of the English Theatre. If we could have a close season for Shakespearean production lasting several years, we would all feel better for it—Shakespeare too.

*

ELEVEN

TECHNIQUE

SEE PAGES 28-30

If I had known when I was writing the lecture that I would be holding a "seminar" the following night, I would have left out that paragraph about technique. For either there ought to be more of this stuff or less, probably none. I used to possess a big fat American book, which somebody must have borrowed and kept, that regarded playwriting as a sort of engineering job. There was a standard formula that applied to everything from *The Trojan Women* to *Getting Gertie's Garter*. This nonsense would do a young writer more harm than good. Others, like William Archer's *Play-Making*, Granville Barker's *Dramatic Method*, C. K. Munro's *Watching a Play*, and the two mentioned in the text (and this is no bibliography, just a random list), could do little harm and might prove most useful.

How much can be taught? I don't know, never having been either teacher or pupil. Probably the chief value of a course like the famous one run by Baker at Harvard was not so much in the actual instruction as in the mutual criticism of the class itself, encouraging everybody to be highly conscious of dramatic problems. The creation of an elaborate *mystique* of play construction and theatrical technique is generally associated not with great imaginative dramatists but with second-rate men making the most of their inside knowledge and experience, the types who used to be "play doctors." On the other hand, I must confess I have always been surprised at the way in which so many clever writers, without theatrical experience, seem to lose all common sense when they try their hands at a play. The enterprise seems to go to their heads. They will submit, as a three-act play, a script that would not occupy the stage half-an-hour. They will introduce, for a scene lasting five minutes, a set that would take thirty men twenty minutes to erect. They will demand impossibilities of everybody. And when clever people can be as silly as this, I am certain it means that the Theatre is not for them; they are just not holding it in their minds at all. The people who will one day write good plays may at first make a number of minor technical mistakes, but as a rule they have the general *feel* of the thing, are in fact beginning to work simultaneously on the two levels.

Some personal notes may not be out of place here. I was very fond of the Theatre as a youth, and in my middle teens I even had thoughts of becoming an actor; but during the later period, nearly ten years, when I was writing for a living but had not begun to write plays, I cannot say I was specially devoted to the Theatre, was always attending it, reading and thinking about it. After the age of seventeen I never had a "stage-struck" period when everything about the Theatre fascinated me. And at no time since I turned dramatist have I ever led the life of the successful man of the Theatre—attending first nights, rushing round dressing-rooms, sending telegrams to everybody, exchanging gossip at late supper parties, generally behaving like a young actress who has made her first hit. When for the time being I have finished *working* in the Theatre, I want to get away from it, to be out of its atmosphere. Its famous "glamour" worked best for me about 1911, when I used to queue outside the gallery door of the Theatre Royal, Bradford, and watch, with wonder and joy touched with envy, the actors on their way to the stage door, with their trilbies perched on their brilliantined curls, their outrageous overcoats barely clearing the ground, fabulous beings far removed from the wool trade. It was then and there, and never again, I took my portion of honeydew and the milk of paradise. The Theatre to which I went to work, twenty years later, was something quite different.

My first job, for which I had had no real preparation, was to collaborate with Edward Knoblock in dramatising my novel *The Good Companions*. Knoblock had done a lot of this work; he was the "play doctor" type. From him I learnt a number of useful technical points—to delay an entrance here, to hurry an exit there, and so forth—but I made a discovery that was more important. We had a scene at the end—I think it was my idea originally but will not swear to it—showing Oakroyd boarding the liner that would take him to his daughter in Canada, so fulfilling his heart's desire. And for this short scene I refused to write any dialogue. What with the liner hooting, our orchestra playing, the audience cheering and clapping, I argued, no dialogue could be heard. And if the scene was not as uproarious as that, if it needed dialogue, then it should not be there at all. Knoblock did not agree, and when I still persisted, he appealed to our manager and producer, Julian Wylie, who strongly supported him. They were old hands, I was a new boy, I must be reasonable, and so forth. But I would not give in: for once I knew in my bones I was right and they were wrong. So, with much shaking of older and wiser heads, the scene went in exactly as I wanted it, with not a word of dialogue. And what happened was exactly what I had told them would happen: the liner hooted, the orchestra played, the audience cheered and clapped, a little man walked up a gangway into a big ship. I decided then that at times, when my imagination was hard at work, when I felt excited about what I was doing, I might have an instinct, an insight, an intuition, worth more than years of experience and a knowledge of all the technical tricks.

So I wrote, at great speed after much brooding over the subject, a play called *Dangerous Corner*, which the daily paper critics did not like. Neither did Knoblock, for I remember running into him, at the back of the circle, on the second or third night, and he was tittering away at my confused attempt to work independently, without his experience and knowledge of what to do and what not to do, and hardly bothered to hide his derision when he caught sight of me. (This suggests he was an unpleasant fellow, which in general he was not; indeed, he was courteous, amiable, helpful; but there was in him a certain feline malice that the Theatre, a notably successful tempter, brought out and sharpened). But the play, by no means my own favourite, has been running somewhere ever since, literally from the Arctic to the Amazon, so I could have had, if I had wanted it, the last titter. Perhaps Knoblock's odd behaviour that night—for he was neither stupid nor ill-mannered—was really defensive; he was an old-fashioned technician, whose Theatre was fast going; so his tittering was a kind of whistling in the dark.

As I write this, I have behind me quarter of a century's work in the Theatre, and there are few tricks of the trade I do not know. With what result? I have to plan and plot far more carefully than I did twenty years ago; I write at about half the speed; I have to re-write whole scenes where once I might not have changed a hundred words in a complete script; and even then I commit blunders and fall into traps I would have once avoided with ease. And this has nothing to do with any general loss of energy and failure of ability: it applies only to my playwriting. With all this experience and technical knowledge supporting me, it takes me far longer to write a play, and I do it with far more sense of difficulty than I used to do when I lacked this experience and knowledge. The reason, I suggest, is this: that for various reasons I no longer have the deep emotional drive towards creation in the Theatre that I had once, and that without this terrific impetus I find it far more difficult to work quickly and surely on both those necessary levels at once. This simultaneous working demands a greater release of energy than my present attitude towards the Theatre is likely to bring me. Do not mistake me: I am not crying stinking fish! The plays are all right when I have finished them. But all my experience and all the technical skill I have acquired down the years bring me less—even on their own level—than was once magically bestowed upon me by my desire to conquer the Theatre.

If I were addressing a class of young writers of prose drama, I would say to them: "Above all, try to avoid a constant dribble of not very important speech, like conversation at a dinner party. It is this more than anything else that makes intelligent people think our prose drama so banal and boring. Don't behave towards the audience as if you were a polite hostess and felt compelled to keep going some sort of dialogue. As long as it is obvious your characters are up to something, allow them at times to be silent or at least laconic. And if they are not feeling very much, then severely ration their words. But then, when they are carried away by emotion, let them be eloquent, give them a fat juicy thumping good speech, as rich as the character can stand. More silent actions, more terse bare speeches cut to the bone, more sudden explosions into eloquence—yes, more of all these, and less and less and less of semi-polite, semi-explanatory talk, neither terse nor eloquent, stuff not coming from the brain nor from the heart but from social conscientiousness, party talk. But don't imagine if you can work this, you have a play. You still need people, and people involved in a significant action. But given the people, given the significant action, this method of handling dialogue will rid you of that woolly, bumbling, buzzy effect, that conventional dinner-party atmosphere, which is what most of our critics are really complaining about. It is the absence of this effect, this atmosphere, in the work of the best Americans that encourages these critics to over-praise them. What they don't spot in this American work, either because they don't want to or because their ears aren't good enough, are the false notes of violence-at-all-costs and cheap-slang-suddenly-turning-into-self-conscious-fine-writing. Also, they don't know how much harder it is for us mumbling, hate-a-scene-old-boy English to write exciting realistic plays about ourselves. However, that is our problem, not theirs. And now, children, our next subject for discussion —the same time here on Thursday—will be one that these critics run away from as hard as they can go, either because they are afraid of it or genuinely believe (quite wrongly) it is no concern of theirs—namely, the proper organisation of the Theatre, without which, no matter how we labour here to improve ourselves, sooner or later we cannot exist. Class dismissed!"

TWELVE

THEATRE-IN-THE-ROUND

A FINAL NOTE

SEE PAGES 30–31

In the lecture I say "If I were beginning again"; but I
will tell you a secret. I like to make some pretence of
modesty in the spoken word, otherwise I would have said
straight out, as I do here now, that it is not a question of
beginning again. Give me, to do what I like with, an
arena playhouse of this sort, within a mile or so of Picca-
dilly Circus, and I will undertake to run it, to write for it,
and to put it indelibly on the map not only of the English
but also of the world Theatre. It should seat about five
hundred persons, have an arena-stage about thirty feet
in diameter, a first-class lighting system, all the usual
offices and amenities, and be so built that in the hidden
gallery where the electricians work it is possible to move
and to operate television cameras. It will not have to be
specially built; that kind of money will not be involved.
What is needed is the basement or ground floor, if it is high
enough, of an existing West End building, suitable for
adaptation. Seats for five hundred people take up surprisingly little room when they run almost all round the

89

stage instead of facing one edge of it. Some years ago I had a plan drawn, roughly to my specification but with the architect making allowance for all the L.C.C. regulations about exits and so forth, and I was delighted to discover from it how comparatively small and compact such a playhouse could be. You could create the whole thing for less than it costs now merely to mess about with the upper circle and gallery of one of our older West End theatres.

If the rich ever read anything I write, they never let me know; but I am hoping this will catch the eye of some man who has money to invest and does not see why he should not have some fun with it. I am not trying to save his soul. I am not asking him to interest himself in art; I will look after the art. I am offering him as good an investment as the City is likely to offer him this year, together with more entertainment that its investment will bring him. We can talk figures in private; but to lure him into that privacy let me point out here that the arena-theatre I have in mind will have lower running costs than an ordinary theatre, it can change productions with the minimum of trouble and expense, it can have any performance televised without having to wreck the ordinary production and to keep out the usual paying audience, and it can soon charm and hold people, once it has overcome their initial scepticism, by its exciting intimacy, its imaginative quality, its concentration upon what is essential Theatre.

And if you ask me what this has to do with The Art of the Dramatist, I must reply: "A great deal. Only it belongs to Part Two of the subject—What To Do With

Your Play When You Have Written It." Which means that somehow we have passed the end of Part One, on which I undertook to lecture, so we must bring these discursive notes to a close.